# OUT OF THE JAR
## MY BOOK OF POEMS

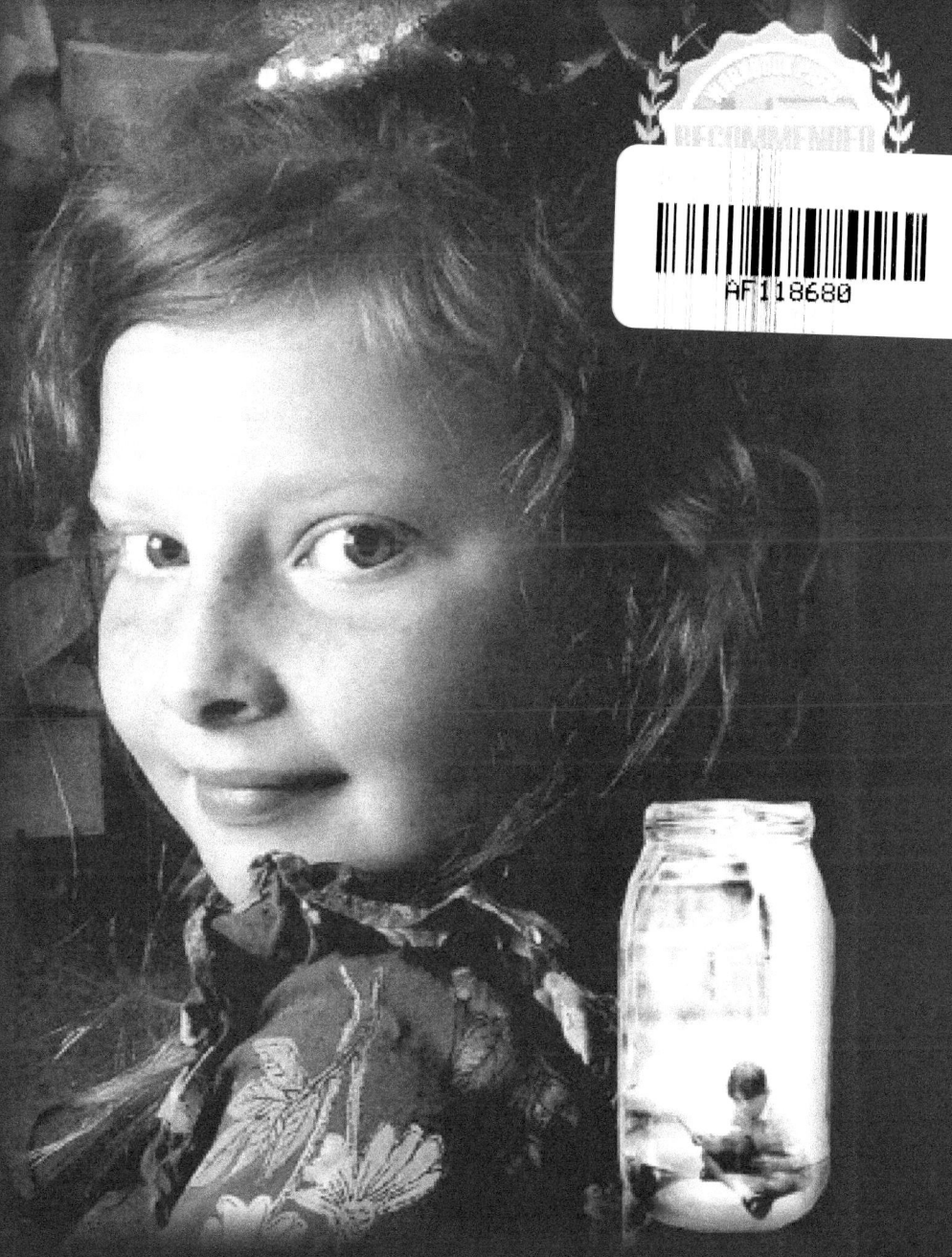

## STEPHEN ROBERT SUTTON

Copyright @2021 by Stephen Robert Sutton

All rights reserved. No part of this book may be reproduced in any form or by any electronic or mechanical means, including information storage and retrieval systems, without permission in writing from the publisher, except by reviewers, who may quote brief passages in a review.

This publication contains the opinions and ideas of its author. It is intended to provide helpful and informative material on the subjects addressed in the publication. The author and publisher specifically disclaim all responsibility for any liability, loss or risk, personal or otherwise, which is incurred as a consequence, directly or indirectly, of the use and application of any of the contents of this book.

Illustrations of this book was created by Mr Stephen Sutton

WORKBOOK PRESS LLC
187 E Warm Springs Rd,
Suite B285, Las Vegas, NV 89119, USA

| | |
|---|---|
| Website: | https://workbookpress.com/ |
| Hotline: | 1-888-818-4856 |
| Email: | admin@workbookpress.com |

Ordering Information:
Quantity sales. Special discounts are available on quantity purchases by corporations, associations, and others. For details, contact the publisher at the address above.

ISBN-13:    978-1-956017-23-6 (Paperback Version)
            978-1-956017-24-3 (Digital Version)

REV. DATE: 03.08.2021

# OUT OF THE JAR:

# MY BOOK OF POETRY

By: Mr. Stephen Robert Sutton

# INTRODUCTION

This book is a collection of my poetry over the years inspired by the life I have led, working in the care setting and travelling all over the world. I hope you enjoy my work and may find it useful to use in the right settings, for instance 'Those in grief' has been used in funerals. My life has been rather colourful to say the least and I have been in a few situations, facing danger and adventure bringing me to the present day. Now at sixty-three I can reflect on this and laugh at the funny events and sigh with relief at actually surviving other situations. I consider each event as a blip in my life and nothing more, yes, I do have nightmare from my worst experiences as a teenager but I just thank god that I survived to tell the tale.

## TABLE OF CONTENTS

LIFE IN A JAR .......................................... 08

LIFES FIRST BREATH ................................. 09

MOTHER ............................................... 10

PROGRESS OF A FOOL ............................... 11

CASTLES FOR KINGS, DUNGEONS OF THE MIND ....... 13

DEVOTION ............................................. 14

WHO CARES ........................................... 15

FARAWAY GIRL ....................................... 16

WAITING FOR YOU ................................... 17

THOSE IN GRIEF ...................................... 18

THE LOST POET ....................................... 19

MY FRIEND THE BOTTLE ............................. 21

CRACKED PORCELAIN ................................ 22

DEPRESSION .......................................... 24

HOPELESS MESS ...................................... 25

BEING OLD ............................................ 27

FACING DESTINY ..................................... 28

CURSED ............................................... 29

WITCHES .............................................. 31

EIGHT SKULLS OF TEVERSHAM ...................... 33

AGAINST THE WIND .................................. 35

| | |
|---|---|
| EMILY IN ECSTASY | 36 |
| GHOSTLY | 37 |
| SIENNA THE VAMPIRE | 38 |
| JUST LIKE MAGIC | 39 |
| GENDER CRISES | 41 |
| SCARS | 42 |
| BE RULED BY ME | 43 |
| BETRAYAL | 44 |
| CADENCE | 45 |
| FALSE HOPE | 47 |
| MADAM MCCAW | 48 |
| LOVE ON THE DOLE | 49 |
| THEN CAME THE NIGHT | 50 |
| IS THIS THE WAY I SHOULD FEEL | 51 |
| JEREMY'S DREAM | 53 |
| KNOW YOUR WORTH | 54 |
| THE OBSERVER | 55 |
| THE OBSERVER PART TWO | 56 |
| TAKE CARE | 57 |
| LAST CARESS | 58 |
| JUST ANOTHER MASQUERADE | 59 |
| DIARY OF A TEENAGE DRUG ADDICT | 60 |
| LUCID LUCY | 61 |

| | |
|---|---|
| ABSOLUTELY ABSTRACT | 62 |
| MY LOQUACIOUS BIRD | 63 |
| MY CADAVEROUS WOMAN | 64 |
| THE BEGUILER | 65 |
| THE TREE | 66 |
| OUTSIDE THE JAR | 68 |
| FOLLOWING THE KING | 70 |
| SCHOOL DAZE | 73 |
| THE JOURNEY | 75 |
| CALM WATERS | 76 |
| SHIELD OF LOVE | 77 |
| PRISONER | 78 |
| CRACKED PORCELAIN – KILLER QUEEN | 79 |

# LIFE IN A JAR

This is a prison of life's long pain
As for the meaning let me explain
People suffer from anxiety and fame
Some are blind, deaf and some are lame
Without all these things they would go very far
Until this time, they must live in a jar

Fame restricts you from the freedom to move
Make plans for the future that they disapprove
A clear direct guided by fools around
Controlled like a robot without any sound
You live every day in a jar
A lost identity you don't know who you are

The title is ambiguous as you can see
But it expresses all things to me
Whether you are ill or just a star
Just remember you live in a jar
Who said your world is an oyster expression like that?
Must have been crazy or some sort of Pratt

# LIFE'S FIRST BREATH

Echoes of laughter

Or cups of joy

The beginning of life

For a girl or a boy

A wonderful moment

You can clearly see

From the very start

Of wonders to be

From life's first breath

Or the first beat of the heart

With close companions

Who will never depart

For trial and error

Will teach us the way

Learn from our mistakes

From day to day

# MOTHER

Comfort me open your heart

And remember me when we are apart

You gave birth to me though I cannot remember

On a winters day deep in December

As I grew up we came closer together

Our bond of unity lasts forever and ever

The closer I get the more that I feel

Is it a dream? No it's certainly real

You comfort me when I am wounded inside

You shelter me when I have nowhere to hide

I treasure these memories like playing in the sand

Or country walks holding your hand

I like Sunday meals and all that you cook

Those bedtime stories that you read from a book

Mother stay with me here what I say

Don't ever leave me until your dying day

## PROGRESS OF A FOOL

From a bastard child you begin to grow
Learned all the things you needed to know
About how to steal a loaf of bread
And forget all the things your mother had said
You knew how to hate, you knew how to lie
Take the path of fate and know how to die
Death and destruction you brought on yourself
By treading on others to gain your own wealth
So die like a fool, for here is your end
You will die alone and without a friend
Even yourself you begin to hate
Showing your feeling now it's too late
Your dying hour, others will never forget
They were right, they won they're bet
They said you would regret the things you have done
And as you die a new life begun
For as one life ends another will start
Lets hope they are better with warmth in their heart.

# CASTLES FOR KINGS, DUNGOENS OF THE MIND

Listen to my voice as it wastes away the hours

Talking about senseless things, like wizards and lizards

Trapped within towers

What pointless words I speak on this very day

And hope that you hear them, though you are far away

My mind is so confused with thoughts and wild things

Of jesters, knights of queens and kings

Oh what waste less hours, what a pointless day

What a boring life, that all I can say

Castles for kings, dungeons of the mind

I feel so trapped here, I am helpless and blind

These chains are my bondages forever I fear

But when sunrise approaches I still feel you near

## DEVOTION

I sacrifice my life for you

I promise to be humble and true

All else I will set apart

And to you I give you my heart

With charity of mind, I devote myself to you

Please observe I am humble and true

You and I will surely understand

That is why I ask for you hand

That we may be one from this day

And let everyone witness what we say

Our vows to be humble and true

You will love only me and I will love only you

And by our devotion we will strive to be

In perfect loving harmony

For richer for poorer better or worse

Join hands and hope that our love lasts the course

No one will divide us our strength shall remain

Listen to my word as I speak so plain

As sure as the ocean will never part

I give my devotion and my heart

## WHO CARES

Who cares about the problems that occurs everyday?
Who cares about the poverty or the pressures of the day?
Who cares about the starving people when riches are your gain?
Who cares about the unemployed I ask you once again
Who cares about the lonely who need some company?
Who cares about the hungry when you wonder what's for tea
Who cares about the young who are growing everyday?
Who cares about their future or when they are going to play?
Who cares about the old when they are frail and weak?
Who care about the humble who cares about the meek?

# FAR AWAY GIRL

My days seem so misty and blue
Was it me that left or was it you?
My life is so strange and confused
I feel so rejected and abused
Coping with my life is a problem you see
Am I still in a prison? Or am I free
What will this world offer me now?
Who will I love, will we meet and how?
We were divided in difference you see
But I often think was it you or was it me
How can I possibly take all the blame?
Perhaps we were too much the same
My mind is causing me too much pain
Is it just me am I going insane?
I have been lonely for much too long
Who could ever say too much is wrong
I try to understand more each day
But the past is so misty so far away
I once loved you that's all I can say
But now we are apart you are so far away

## WAITING FOR YOU

I sit at home and wait for you to call

I am so confused I am writing on a wall

I have written your name a thousand times or more

I have written it right across the door

Tis foolish of me to think she will return

When living her life is really her concern

But I will sit here what more can I do

And spend my time thinking just of you

So I wait at home just waiting for you

Surely our life together is not really through

I lost you many years ago

We were divided by differences you know

We grew apart over a short time to me

Now we are apart at least one of us is free

In my heart I want you I feel this yearn

Please be with me I want you to return

## THOSE IN GRIEF

Wipe a tear from a mourning eye

And please remember I wanted to die

My life seemed to last so many years

So don't cry don't shed any tears


Open your eyes raise your head

Its not your fault that I am dead

I loved you dearly with all my heart

So be not sad now we're apart


I drank to you my last farewell

And left you fresh flowers for you to smell

I left a rose pressed in a book

Near a verse please take a look


I'm happy now I rest in peace

My painful body had to cease

Now at last I am free from pain

You are able to live again

## THE LOST POET

The poet writes his final line
With his memory deep inside
Experience mixed within his dreams
With thoughts he could not hide

Hidden away in a fortress tower
So high upon a hill
Lost within his solitude
With dreams he could not fulfill

A trapped talent within a cell
Within your mind fresh thoughts do dwell
A man that is trapped within his mind
Here the lost poet may dwell

Always thinking of the people you create
When your asleep new dreams you motivate
Like a person within a person
Fictitious people within a dream
Nightmares make you awake
And no one will here you scream

The poet writes his final line
Of a person without a friend

The conclusion is written on this day
The poet must come to an end

So daylight is over
Darkness will end the day
The candles are gone they burned so low
So you must lose your way
And the dreams inside your mind have all gone
Just as the hot sun melts the snow
And as the winter disappears
You must leave this life and go

The poet writes his final line
With his memory deep inside
Experience mixed within his dreams
With thoughts he could not hide

Hidden away in a fortress tower
So high upon a hill
Lost within his solitude
With dreams he could not fulfill
The poet writes his final line about things that couldn't be
Lived his life within a dream the poet writes his final line for me

# MY FRIEND THE BOTTLE

Drink a glass of wine with me
Drink it down instead of tea
Drink a toast to your lost friends
Have another till the bottle ends

My friend the bottle is always by my side
My friend the bottle knows when to hide
My friend the bottle is close at hand
My friend the bottle is always in demand

So drink to my health
Drink to my wealth
Drink to the birth of a child
Drink until you're reckless and wild
Drink to a new life to begin
Drink whiskey or even neat gin

But then stop, be in control
Don't lose your character or public role
Think of others who may get hurt
Why roll in the gutter or even in dirt
Are you that desperate to sink so low?
Or have you the will power to just say no

# CRACKED PORCELAIN

### CRACKED PORCELAIN

You were just like porcelain to me

With smooth skin perfect as can be

I kept you clean and free from flaws

Like my ornaments I kept you indoors

The image that I had of you

Was perfection and love that grew

But then my porcelain mask had gone

The colourful image that once shone

Defiled by others with a shameless grin
You had become cracked porcelain


Once you had been a model child
Now you are just crazy and wild
I nurtured a victim of child abuse
Now I could never let my daughter loose


The world turned its back on your beautiful face
Leaving you in such a disgrace
Defiled by others with a shameless grin
Now I know your cracked porcelain

# DEPRESSION

In a dark place far from what I know

In a place so dismal where most fear to go

I linger alone far from my thoughts

Like a leper or a skin full of warts

Like a body disfigured by societies cruel tricks

I am in a bad way, I 'm in a fix

It's hard to explain my feelings you see

This isn't my way this isn't me

I don't eat in the day or show my face

I walk with my head down all over the place

Time passes by me I know not the hour

I am like a machine that has lost all its power

I go deeper and deeper in a dark pit

I don't care about life I don't give a shit

Without taking these pills I would surely be dead

Please help me escape from what lies ahead

## HOPELESS MESS

What sense is there in clouding your mind?
By destroying yourself, are you so blind?
You consume such stuff in your head
By the time you are twenty you will surely be dead
You pollute your body and strain your brain
You live in a box close to a drain

You sit by the roadside with your head in a bag
And manage a breath between each rolled up fag
You drink from a bottle shared by a few
But as for clear thinking it's not up to you

Your dirty mouth keeps people away
You had better start living in a new kind of way
Come out of that dustbin you look such a mess
Change your image and become a success
Dope will never help you to find a job or career
But it will end your life within a year

Empty lives produce empty dreams
Shallow heads without any schemes
Wisdom belongs to those who can think
Haggled brains for those who can drink
So wake up when this nightmare ends
Who needs reality and who needs friends?
Logical thinking is far from your mind
Conquer your prison, you are confined
You are a tramp a modern day drop out
You are a mess of this I don't doubt
Your future died when you were asleep
Now the frail weak body lies dead in a heap

# BEING OLD

Take away the pressure
That comes of being old
And just leave me the pleasure
That's as pure to me as gold

Light a dozen candles
And watch me glow so bright
Each flame is like a memory
Remember me tonight

These wrinkles on my face
My hair is going grey
All that is left are my memories
Thoughts of yesterday

The songs I still remember
So clear from the start
But then my memories fail me
I forget the second part

# FACING DESTINY

I feel at peace

Within my soul

Now at last

My mind is whole

For life's great pleasures are no longer mine

I no longer feel my body entwined

By problems of how I must be fed

Or how long will I sleep alone in my bed

I saw my destiny within my mind

I felt myself in ecstasy examining my find

So now I look up to you with my mind clear and bright

I look down on the world like a star shining light

# CURSED

## CURSED

Spirits of the past do see

A curse on a family

Mirrors just to see through

Like a gateway they come for you


Snakes, spiders and creatures come

To menace you when the curse begun

Voices crying out in fear
Touching you when they are near


Swamps devour you when you wake
Waters drown you in a lake
Fire consumes you in this hour
Or poison to your lips so sour


Deadly is the curse at night
You wake up screaming with a fright
Who knows what terror lies within?
As the mirror reveals its mighty Sin

# WITCHES

## WITCHES

Witches fly high in the air

Witches dance without a care

They cast their spells late at night

And dance around under the moonlight

Witches cauldrons bubbling with the fire

They dance around and never tire

With cackling sounds they make a fright
Like owls that hoot throughout the night

Witches display magic at night
What a display, an awesome sight
Trick after trick, spell after spell
An incredible sight didn't they do well

Dark witches are legends white witches too
Showing the world all they can do
Halloween is the night for them
They can keep appearing again and again

## EIGHT SKULLS OF TEVERSHAM

## EIGHT SKULLS OF TEVERSHAM

This is a tale of witches or a legend to me
Told of a family from Teversham you see
The horrors and evil which I will unfold
Of murderous dark witches the story is told

The night when the witches evil did slay
Their wicked magic struck on their prey
Eight witches came forth into the night
Killed a young family who couldn't fight

A young boy called Eric swore revenge to them all
By forming an army and the witches would fall
Eight skulls was his trophy to hand to the mayor
Proof of their deaths that he must now share

Death to dark witches and descendants too
Eight more skulls he collected before he was through
But eight had a meaning that the witches new well
It means resurrection as part of a spell

So the witches linger in a cave far away
In a place in Scotland that where they will stay

## AGAINST THE WIND

How weak I feel against the wind

That rages against me like a raging man

Forces me back so fierce

While I do what I can

With the strength of a bull

And as fast as a cheetah

Faster and fast but I beat you

Unbearably cold and pushed back with the rain

Harder and harder I can hardly explain

Bravely I battle its heartless gain

Getting wetter and wetter due to the rain

On and on I endure the pain within

Onward I go and finally win

# EMILY IN ECSTASY

Thoughts that a restless mind
An imagination of a different kind
Thoughts float like a stream in time
And travel along like an endless rhyme
Thinking of things you used to say
Relaxing so peacefully at the end of the day

And like a sparrow in winter you find a place to rest
To a place of solitude where you make your nest
You prepare yourself for each season to start
Ever more loving with warmth in your heart
But who is that woman people ask me
I reply its Emily who lives in ecstasy

# GHOSTLY

Spirits of an evening rise

And you won't believe your eyes

As here before you crystal clear

Ghostly presence they come near

By chance within a haunted house

They appear and some do pounce

Restless souls linger through the night

And present themselves like an awesome sight

They haunt you in the dark of night

And make you jump giving you a fright

And to the break of dawn

You are startled to the morn

# SIENNA THE VAMPIRE
# BLOOD TRAIL-ACROSS TIME

Running through a forest fearful of her life

Sheltered by the trees at night in a dreadful strife

The vampire is alone hunted like a dear

Running through the clearing

There she shall appear

Sheltered in a castle in a darkened room

There she finds a picture in which she is consumed

She falls out of the picture and lands upon a floor

Falls upon an observer close beside a door


This begins her story this is what's foretold

From out of a time portal in this time is told

A vampire from another age desperately seeking a friend

But what is her destiny what is written in the end

# JUST LIKE MAGIC

It all began in Chantell's play room one day

She heard the voice of a child as she began to play

Alicia called out from her world

It was a call for help

Chantell's reaction was very clear

She let out a cry like a yelp

She entered a mirror into her world

Not knowing what I would find

To my surprise this other world

Had put me in a bind

A magic world, a fantasy world

Such a different place

With unicorns and witches

Amongst a different race

# JUST LIKE MAGIC

# GENDER CRISES

Who am I, I don't know

Am I female or just for show?

Am I a person who thinks and walks?

Or a man who just thinks and talks

Am I a person who questions my thoughts?

Alters my body from all marks and warts

Am I so weak or am I so strong

Is it a problem or am I so wrong?

I watch my body I see it change

Is this unusual or is it so strange

Who am I and what is my sex

What is my gender and is it the best?

I want some answers please let me know

Give me some guidance let my life flow

## SCARS

Be who you want to be

Do what you want to do

Live how you want to live

It's up to you


Forget what you need to forget

It's all in the past

Live for the present

It's with you at last


The scars do remind you

Of your past life that has been

Some scars are hidden

They will never be seen


Plan for your future

trips far ahead

But don't dream about them

You can't reach them from your bed

# BE RULED BY ME

Don't ever let people

Tell you how to walk

Don't even let them

Tell you how to talk


Be your own person

You know you can

Do what you want to

Do what you can


Be independent

Take your own advice

Do what you want

As long as you're nice


Parents will guide you

Take hold of your hand

Try not to be lonely

But that's not a command

Be what you want to be

Hear what I say be ruled by me

# BETRAYAL

In the dawning following the night

I will speak about a plight

The one we shall discuss

Is non other than Jesus

For what has come to be

Was foretold from history

From the scriptures old

This is what I was told

A man would be betrayed

His life would not be saved

A sacrifice he would make

Of his life god would take

He was to save mankind

That was on his father's mind

And so the betrayal took place

When Judas kissed his masters face

Some may betray us this way

The example remains for us today

# CADENCE

Please spare a little time
Just for my little rhyme
That dances on the page
And never seems to age
It has a cadence style
That travels all the while
It lightens up your day
Its nice in every way

Going up and down with sound
Like music all around
It is jolly it is fun
As bright as the sun

It warms and pleases
Without any diseases
Short and sweet
Unlike granddads feet

It smiles through the day

It is funny in every way

So listen out loud

While it travels through a cloud

Then falls with the rain


How can I explain

Watch for yourself

Sitting on a shelf

And watch it fall

Getting very small

This is so

Now go

## FALSE HOPE

Don't clutch at straws or live in false hope
You're just fooling yourself pretending to cope
With desires and pleasures far from your grasping fingers
Holding onto false hope until nothing lingers
You sit all alone with false hope till this day
Then years go by and your life fades away

Now you are aging you now see your mistake
You kept all your candles on a dream wedding cake
False hope was your downfall your cause has now failed
You're left alone in your life the ship has sailed
You stand at the harbour your boat sails in the distance
Now you remain in a lonely existence
So you have learned a lesson don't try to cope
By dreams or by schemes don't live in false hope

# MADAM McCAW

Madam McCaw is a dreadful bore
Who pries into your life
She talks and talks nags and nags
Take care she is never your wife


Madam McCaw she knows the law
She studies it every night
She stays up with you till the early hours
And she does this just for spite


Madam McCaw could be young or old
Who nags you to your grave
She could be watching you right now
So make sure that you behave

## LOVE ON THE DOLE

A strange romance is in the air
As you walk about without a care
For what is the point of feeling kind
For life is so empty and blind
For standing before you in a long queue
Is a beautiful girl looking at you?
She seems so shy looks at you with a glance
So you surprise her and ask for a dance
You take her to one side so no one can hear
And she blushes because you stand so near
Then you ask for a date
She replies this must be fate
Now you are successful you have reached your goal
This is a happy day its love on the dole

# THEN CAME THE NIGHT

I love the day

To my only delight

I live out my day

Then came the night


My life fades away

When it is twilight

I leave the day

Then came the night


I give you my ears

I loose my sight

It's very clear

Then came the night


I have my dreams

Lost under starlight

I ended my days

Then came the night

# IS THIS THE WAY I SHOULD FEEL?

Is this the way I should feel?

Is this the way I should feel?

When I argue in a room with paper thin walls

Run out of the room and slam all the doors

Is this the way I should feel?

I ask you

Is this the way I should feel?


When I love her so much but fear her touch

When she is so kind is it all in my mind?

Is this the way I should feel?

When life seems a joke and I laugh out loud

I know its unusual when I enter a crowd

Is this the way I should feel?

I ask you

Is this the way I should feel?

When someone tells lies

And I just close my eyes

Ignoring the fact

I know I should react

Or be ignorant or lazy

Be foolish or crazy


Dangerous or rich

Or fall down a ditch

And forget the entire world

Yes, why not forget this world

Is this the way I should feel?

I ask you

Is this the way I should feel?

# JEREMY'S DREAM
# (DREAM OF A DISABLED PERSON)

Come with me and journey a mind
Examine the facts and look at my find
Jeremy's dream is so complex and true
Think of it this way it could have been you

It began with a thought of reincarnation
A misunderstanding so much complication
Jeremy's past was very real
No one could explain the way he must feel

His handy cap prevents him from speaking
The only sound he can make is high pitched screeching
Who can explain? Nobody can
About Jeremy's past
As a near perfect man

# KNOW YOUR WORTH

Can you value yourself?

Do you know your own worth?

Did you have a price tag?

Present at your own birth?

Have you been weighed?

To know your own worth

Balanced on scale like gold

Or the salt of the earth


Keep your price high

Balance things right

Be kind to all people

Be everyone's delight

Your qualifications are gathered

Over the years

So be confident at all times

Get rid of your fears

Your own personality

Is a qualification alone

Know your worth

You are one on your own

## THE OBSERVER

The observer sits and admires the view

He watches me and he watches you

He sees every move you make

He even observes the steps you take


He is never far with his watchful eye

He remains with you until you die

He observes every breath you take

And even observes every mistake


You cannot see this observer you see

Because he is invisible to you and me

But one thing is certain as life course you do take

He will always protect you and keep you safe

He has qualifications of a perfect man

And he has been here since life first began.

## THE OBSERVER –PART TWO

Life is much greater than you and me
He controls the wind and the rain
And parted the sea

He observes the earth, moon and heavens above
He is so might so full of love
The observer created all things you see
From creatures on the land and those in the sea

His knowledge is great his mind is supreme
He even observes the things that we dream
He knows and loves you even when you are wrong
And when you're in trouble he will help you along
So observe for yourself how he wants you to be
Then we can live in perfect harmony

## TAKE CARE

At the end of a letter
I take time to prepare
I reflect on the past
And sincerely say take care

When people part
For a journey they prepare
Their final words to their friend
Is take care

When lovers are parted
On a journey somewhere
They treasure their words
And say take care

Grand parents or children
Families with love in the air
Families reunite and just say take care

So read a nice letter with thought and with care
A cheerful letter that ends with take care

## LAST CARESS

Gently the night came a red moonlit sky

I caught your tears as you began to cry

They flowed gently through my fingertips

Then into your mouth and moistened your lips

They failed to tell me of this time when we would be so close

About the pain and medication just an adequate dose

How I wish this last caress would last forever more

But life is hard and its now time to lose the one you adore

We talk about such silly things anything but death

Till she fell asleep in my arms and took her final breath

## JUST ANOTHER MASQUERADE

I watch your face and your eyes do tell
The person within the odd outer shell
But deception may cause a person to fade
In a cunning masquerade

He conceals all the secrets to the depth of his past
And is joined by others like players well cast
A theatrical tableaux is set before your eyes
It's a mass deception of cruelty and lies

They travel about from cities far and wide
With marvels around you with tricks on their side
So be wary of these who want to be paid
Its just another masquerade

# DIARY OF A TEENAGE DRUG ADDICT

I wake up this morning with my hair in a mess
I can't help it oh I couldn't care less
Yesterday was better I don't know why
I feel dreadful I just want to die

Just the other day I had a dream
It was far out I had to scream
A week a ago I heard of a death
I have memories of her
It's all that's left
A single flower floats in a gutter
What a sad loss is all I can mutter

Cry after cry is all that I hear from my hospital bed
Another mind is empty gone out of his head
Pink red and orange is all I can see
Wont someone help me please set me free

## *LUCID LUCY*

Lucid Lucy lean and juicy

Can you understand?

Why I love you naughty Lucy

May I hold your hand?

Lucid Lucy just eats muesli

For breakfast lunch and tea

Tell me Lucid Lucy will you marry me?

Lucid Lucy lean and juicy

Let me be your mate

Why shake your head Lucid Lucy

She tells me I am too late

# ABSOLUTELY ABSTRACT

Paint a picture and watch it glow

An abstract image of a fantasy will grow

Images softly inter mingle like mixed thoughts in a dream

Absolutely abstract the best you have ever seen


With circles and stars that will never part

And fine white unicorns that will capture your heart

With dogs, cats and toads we even have mice

We even had spiders that didn't look very nice


Paint many pictures with triangles and squares

Now draw a building with plenty of stairs

Remember old Lowry he painted and then

Produced his likable match stalk men

Paint another picture even more bizarre

Made of odds and end taken from a car

Squares and circles shapes of a kind

Thoughts from elusions conjured up from your mind

Glasses and mirrors reflections of you

There is endless things an artist can do

## MY LOQUACIOUS BIRD

My loquacious bird just likes to be heard

She sings her songs away

Though no one hears her she still wants to sing

All through the summers day

My loquacious bird needs to be heard

Singing so plainly but clear

She knows how to find me and before long she is standing near

My loquacious bird loves to be heard

She sits close beside me I dread

The only time she will shut up is when she's finally dead

# MY CADAVEROUS WOMAN

Oh woman of stone you stand alone

Unique in every way

Your cold and cruel I am so surprise

How do you get through the day?

How I can tell I am in a living hell

Frustrated in every way

I pray to god for sanity to get me through the day

You look at me with a blank expression

Then drive me into a deep depression

For several years you have lived with me

Your only asset is making the tea

I try to survive and have to cope

You promise to leave and I live in hope

How do you get rid of an awful smell?

I dream of throwing her down a well

But fear the ghost that she may be

And just destroy my sanity

So I live to face the day

My cadaverous woman is here to stay

# THE BEGUILER

The beguiler deceives you with love and affection

He attacks you when you have no protection

He tries to fool and amuse

But he only knows how to abuse

With tricks and charms and acts of magic

The end result could be quite tragic

So take heed of my warning and leave his arms

Take nothing from him, not even his charms

His beguilement is treacherous and cruel

His victim is often an innocent fool

Who knows nothing of beguilement, evil and hate?

Listen to me I beg you, before it's too late

Just think of goodness, drive him out of your mind

Reject his beguilement and true love you will find

# TREE

How I wish that I were a tree
With lots of people admiring me
With lots of branches and leave to see
All adorned in my majesty

How I wish I were a tree
With the wind blowing through me
Waving about what a spectacle to see

How I wish I was a tree
What a sight I could be
Standing there for all to see
And no one to answer to just totally free

How I wish I were a tree
How profound that would be
Branches reaching to the sky
Dropping leave on those passing by
And the fruits that I bear
Falling apples everywhere
Or chestnuts dropping on the ground
Isn't it funny and so profound?
Oh how happy I would be if was only a living tree

# THE TREE

# OUTSIDE THE JAR

Life in a jar was a protective zone
Where I lived my life all alone
With dyslexia and asthma keeping me company
Dealing with those now sets me free

Outside to jar is where I dwell
Having left a living hell
The jar was my prisoner I have to tell
From early life was there I fell

I learned to read and write myself
By choosing comics off a shelf
I discovered it was my place to be
By learning a new strategy

The asthma was caused by childhood stress
I could certainly see I was in a mess
I needed to change my state of mind
And leave my painful past behind

I struggled to be who I wanted to be
And now I live in ecstasy
Through education I excelled and now I feel so overwhelmed

# ELVIS PRESLEY

## FOLLOWING THE KING

From a teen in the seventies

I discovered a man

With a fine voice

And I became a fan

They called him the king

Of a rock and roll age

As told by the media

Splashed on a front page

Elvis Presley was a legend

So the papers say

His songs and his movies

Known to this day

I followed his life

From Tupelo to Graceland

I saw almost his entire home

And part of his land

I went to sun records
Followed his musical career

The foundation of his life
And felt him near

Graceland was wonderful
A fine place to see
But the best of the rooms
Was the jungle room for me

# SCHOOL DAZE

Those days of being at school

Showing the teacher, I am no fool

Sat at a desk staring into space

Not being attentive and you could tell by my face

I wasn't listening my concentration was poor

All I wanted was to leave via the door

Art class was fun I could show off my talent and skill

I had a purpose, a role to forfill

Maths was my weakness fractions a chore

The teachers got frustrated they knew the score

I enjoyed English especially poetry

I enjoyed reciting verse it was fun for me

I liked history and French too

Domestic science and all that baloo

I hated being punished it was such a disgrace

Being hit with a ruler or slapped on my face

# SCHOOL DAZE

# THE JOURNEY

Hustle bustle everywhere
People travel without a care
On buses and trains, they have to go
On trams they travel too and fro

In crowded stations all day long
Delays in transport when things go wrong
All hunched up like peas in a pan
Filling the transport wherever they can

Sweaty bodies stand and sit
With bags and cases, they try to fit
Chatting some cursing wildly
Suffocating in such misery

Rude people push their way in a queue
With no manners except for a few
With the sound of children screaming so loud
Please rescue me get me out of this crowd

# CALM WATERS

Calm my heart

Lift my soul

Bring me close

Make me whole


Calm my waters

By the stream

Calm my storm

Within my dream


Trust me with you

Be my mate

Calm my waters

Before it's too late

# SHIELD MY LOVE

Shield me protect me

Comfort my soul

Love me forever

Make me your goal


Cushion my body

Shield my heart

Protect my body

Right from the start


Shield my love

Know how I am feeling

Love how I look

Its so appealing


Happy am I

Happy forever

Now you are with me

Please leave me never

## PRISONER

The sentence is very clear

As in a court you do appear

The judge passes sentence in his own way

And you are condemned on this very day


Into prison you go unhappily along

Reflecting on your crime and what you did wrong

You are alone confined to a cell

This is your home now this is your hell


With mould and graffiti on the walls all around

Dirty and damp life is profound

For your deathly sentence lasts so long

This is your future it's where you belong

# CRACKED PORCELAIN – KILLER QUEEN

I want to be like you
With long hair and eyes of blue
Though sometime your wear a frown
I just realised your eyes are brown

I admire your courage
And you are so free
How I wish I were you
Instead of me

I dress like you
Although I am a man
I walk like a woman
And I do what I can

I would kill for you
And protect your name
I am serious you see
This isn't a game

The people who die
Deserve all they get
I do it for you
To pay a great dept
I follow you
As you go out at night
And stay close by you
Keeping you in my sight

You were a victim
Of abuse in the past
They will not harm you
I will get them at last

I changed my body
To look like you
So many changes

I could be you

# SRS BOOKS

Books available by myself under various names

EIGHT SKULLS OF TEVERSHAM

CRACKED PORCELAIN

FOR THE LOVE OF CHARLOTTE

STORIES BEYOND BELIEF 1 and 2

CURSED

BLOOD TRAIL – ACROSS TIME

CONFLICT OF FAITH

UNDERSTANDING JODIE

OPERATION BRAINSTORM

DOUBLE EXPOSURE

CRACKED PORCELAIN –ACTS OF ABUSE

www.ingramcontent.com/pod-product-compliance
Lightning Source LLC
LaVergne TN
LVHW020431080526
838202LV00055B/5124